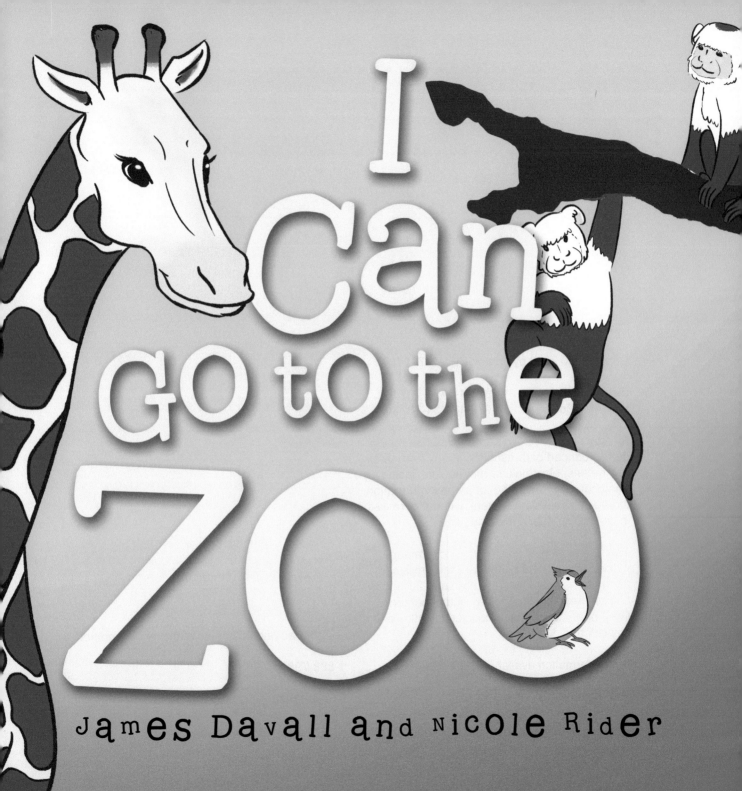

I Can Go to the Zoo

James Davall and Nicole Rider

Print information available on the last page

Rev. date: 01/13/2018

To order additional copies of this book, contact:
Xlibris
1-888-795-4274
www.Xlibris.com
Orders@Xlibris.com

I Can Go to the Zoo

It's Saturday morning and I'm so excited!

My mommy and daddy are taking me to the zoo.

I can't wait to see the animals.

We can see

monkeys.

My favourite animals are elephants. They make me laugh!

We see lions
and tigers.

SNAKE

Snakes and crocodiles.

Look how big
the giraffes are!

Look how small the birds are.

I can go to the
zoo, can you?